# Fun Fashion Trivia

## FAB QUESTIONS FOR THE CHIC AND SAVVY

*by Ree van Dijk*

# Contents


1. The Creators: Designers, Couturiers, & Legends............................5

2. The Influencers: Icons, Models, & Muses .....................................12

3. The Narrators: Editors, Publicists, & Writers .............................19

4. The Artists: Stylists, Painters, Photographers, & Illustrators .....26

5. The Lingo: Words, Terms, & Idioms .............................................33

6. The Institutions: Events, Museums, & Organizations.................40

7. The Moments: Influential, Memorable, & Momentous ...............47

The Answers.......................................................................................52

About the Author ..............................................................................64

From the Author ...............................................................................65

# Contents


1. The Creators: Designers, Couturiers, & Legends............................5

2. The Influencers: Icons, Models, & Muses ......................................12

3. The Narrators: Editors, Publicists, & Writers ..............................19

4. The Artists: Stylists, Painters, Photographers, & Illustrators .....26

5. The Lingo: Words, Terms, & Idioms .............................................33

6. The Institutions: Events, Museums, & Organizations.................40

7. The Moments: Influential, Memorable, & Momentous ...............47

The Answers....................................................................................52

About the Author ............................................................................64

From the Author .............................................................................65

# 1. The Creators: Designers, Couturiers, & Legends

## Level: Easy

1. Which renowned French designer revolutionized women fashion in 1947 with his *Ligne Corolle* aka the *New Look*?

2. Name the alumnus of the prestigious ESMOD, who was appointed as the creative director of the leading fashion house, Balmain in 2011.

3. Which creative director carried on her brother's legacy by maintaining the brand's sexy and glamorous designs including J.Lo's Grammy 2000 tropical green dress.?

4. For her second nuptials in 1968, former first lady Jacqueline Kennedy wore an ivory knee-length dress with a pleated skirt. Who designed this modish wedding dress for her?

5. Which celebrated French designer, known for the *Petite Robe Noire,* started her fashion career as a hat maker and opened her first store in Paris in 1910?

6. Who designed First Lady Michelle Obama's stunning gowns for both the first and second inauguration balls of President Barack Obama?

7. Who does the fashion world have to thank for revolutionizing womenswear in the 70's by designing a popular closet staple; the patterned-jersey Wrap Dress?

8. Name the Tunisian designer who released his unhurried collections in private showings and was nicknamed the King of Cling in the 80's.

9.   Which beloved British designer, sometimes called the l'enfant terrible, won the British Fashion Awards Designer of the Year and the CFDA Best International Designer in 2003?

10.  Name the legendary creative director who is credited with the revival of French fashion empire Chanel after taking the helms in 1982.

11.  Who designed the iconic pink cone bra for Madonna's Blond Ambition tour?

12.  Which eternally youthful, cartwheeling fashion designer won the prestigious Coty Fashion Critics Award at age 29 in 1971?

~

## Level: Intermediate

13.  Name the beloved French designer who introduced the sack dress in the 1950s in collaboration with his mentor, Cristóbal Balenciaga.

14.  Which American couturier co-opted the logos of luxury brands for a decade (1982-1992) to create bespoke outfits which he sold at his Ladies and Gentlemen Boutique in Harlem?

15.  Name the American designer from the Bronx, NY with an eponymous label which started 1967 with mens neckties and later grew into a leading lifestyle brand.

16.  Who got her start as a designer at Anne Klein, and later debuted her own line with the Seven Easy Pieces collection in 1985?

17.  Which Haitian-Italian designer is a former-model and a winner in the Vogue Italia Who Is On Next 2011 competition?

18.  Who designed the iconic wedding dress worn by the Duchess of Windsor in 1937?

19.  Name the American designer and film director who is credited, in part, with the reinvention and financial turnaround of GUCCI after becoming the then struggling brand's creative director in 1994.

20.  In 1953 Jacqueline Bouvier wed then senator John F. Kennedy in an enchanting tissue-silk, off-the-shoulder gown.Who designed this iconic wedding dress?

21. Which British designer was the creative director of Chloé, from 1997 to 2001, and is revered for her stance on and promotion of eco-fashion and sustainability?

22. Which avant-garde Japanese designer collaborated with Adidas to create Y-3?

23. Name the Italian designer who was known for her surrealist designs and for brightening up the fashion scene with the introduction of her favorite hue, "Shocking Pink", in the 1930's.

24. Which American designer founded the Italian luxury brand Off-White in 2014?

~

Level: Advance

25. Name the Belgian designer who was the former assistant of Jean Paul Gaultier and is referred to as Fashion's Invisible Man because of his incredibly low public profile.

26. Which Parisian couturier introduce her signature robe de style in the 1920s?

27. Which Paris-based English couturier founded La Chambre Syndicale De La Confection Et De La Couture Pour Dames Et Fillettes in 1868?

28. In June 1964 Women's Wear Daily published a photo of a model wearing a topless swimsuit called a monokini. Name the designer of that monokini.

29. Name the Dutch avant-garde designer who interned at Alexander McQueen in 2006 and debuted her Chemical Crows collection featuring unconventional materials and 3-D printing in Amsterdam Fashion Week 2007.

30. Who is the self-proclaimed *fashion tyrant* who liberated women from the corset but bound their legs with the hobble skirt in the early 1900s?

31. What was the name of the French fashion house that was opened in 1985 by 4 sisters and was later revered for their daring designs featuring Oriental elements, embroidery and lace?

32. Name the Egypt-born French designer who created the luxury fashion house Chloé in 1952.

33. Which beloved haute-couture child prodigy took the helm as the head designer of Dior in 1957, at the tender age of 21?

34. Name the acclaimed Italian designer  who holds a Ph.D in political science from the University of Milan and who grew the high-end luggage company founded by her grandfather in 1913 into a global luxury brand.

35. Which Italian-born French futuristic designer was expelled from the haute couture guild, Chambre Syndicale, in 1959 for creating ready-to-wear collections? (He was later reinstated).

36. In the 70's a Jerusalem-born British fashion and interior designer influenced the bohemian chic movement in London with a mix of Middle Eastern styles and opulent textiles. Name the designer.

# 2. The Influencers: Icons, Models, & Muses

## Level: Easy

37. A lady of many firsts; name the trailblazing Somali-American model who was the first to wear a hijab to compete in the Miss Minnesota Pageant 2016.

38. Name the model/actress who's career began at age 10 in the most splendid way; being photographed by Bruce Weber for Vogue Italia wearing Philip Treacy hats.

39. Which International top model with a famous Dutch model mom began her career at age 2 as a Guess Kids model?

40. Which beloved lawyer, author, university administrator, and bonafide style icon served as the First Lady of the United States from 2009-2017?

41. Name the  British fashion icon known for her beauty and benevolence who wore a historic 25-foot silk train on her wedding day in July, 1981.

42. Perhaps the ultimate style icon of the 80"s; name the international sensation who's iconic outfits included the sequined white gloves, the gold leotard, military jackets, cropped trousers, and fedoras.

43. Her repertoire includes columnist, photographer, book editor, and polyglot. Name America's First Lady of Style dubbed *"Her Elegance"* by WWD's  John Fairchild.

44. Which Caribbean beauty and award winning singer who uses her platform to champion diversity in fashion and beauty won the CFDA 2014 *Style Icon Award*?

45. Her's was a *nomen est omen,* for this former actress was destined to be the personification of elegance and refinement. Name the icon who not only played a princess onscreen (*The Swan,1956*) but also became one when she married the Prince of Monaco.

46. Name the revered actress, humanitarian, and style icon who served as muse and friend to designer Hubert De Givenchy. Their collaborations include costumes for *Charade* (1963), *Funny Face* (1957), and *Sabrina* (1954).

47. Which model, mogul, and former head of Baby Phat signed a modeling career with Chanel at age 13?

48. According to Forbes Magazine, which famous American model who began her career as a reality star ousted Gisele Bundchen to take the position as the highest-paid model in 2017?

~

Level: Intermediate

49. Name the hat-loving fashion magazine editor and aristocrat who bought Alexander McQueen's entire graduation collection in 1992.

50. Which actor, known for his timeless look of denims paired with a  T-shirt and a leather jacket, achieved cult status as a symbol of youthful rebellion and revelry after his untimely death at 24 years old in 1955?

51. Amongst her many show-stopping, thought-provoking, and iconic fashion ensembles are her Kermit coat (2009) and her sea urchin dress (2014). Name the acclaimed American singer, songwriter, and actress who's stage name was derived from a Queen's 1984 single.

52. Name the New York Socialite, horsewoman, stage actress, and bonafide style icon who authored *First Garden* (1976) and *Tiny Green Thumbs* (2000).

53. Which supermodel and activist who started her career at age 15 was the first Black model on the cover of Time Magazine(1991) and French Vogue (1988)?

54. One of the most recognizable bags in fashion's history bears her name. Name the English-born, actress, singer, and songwriter who starred in the French movie *Slogan* (1969).

55. Which supermodel worn two Daytime Emmy Awards (2008 & 2009) for her eponymous talk show which she hosted and produced?

56.  Name the pop icon who starred in *The Princess and a Showgirl* (1957), a romantic comedy produced by her very own movie production company.

57.  It was reported that her first capsule collection for TopShop in 2007 sold out in one day. Name the supermodel turned designer who was named Forbes second Top Earning Model in 2012 with an earning of $9.2 million.

58.  Which supermodel best known by her mononym, was awarded the CFDA *Fashion Icon Lifetime Achievement Award* in 2010?

59.  Name the musician who lives up to his surname by being a pop fashion icon with his gender-defying ensembles including wearing a dress for the cover of Vogue's December 2020 issue.

60.  Which model known for breaking down barriers within the modeling industry  published the book *A New Model: What Confidence, Beauty, and Power Really Look Like* in 2017?

~

## Level: Advance

61.  What is the professional name of the French model born Simone Michelene Bodin (1925) who served as muse to three of fashion's top luminaries; Jacques Fath, Hubert de Givenchy, and Azzedine Alaia?

62.  Name the Emmy winning American actress and singer who collaborated with Tommy Hilfiger to design a Spring and a Fall collection in 2019.

63.  Which double-amputee athlete-turned-model-turned-actress wore intricately carved prosthetics to walk the unforgettable Alexander McQueen's S/S99 runway?

64.  Name the supermodel/tv host/executive producer who won the German beauty contest *Winning Model '92* at age 18?

65.  He rebelled against the status quo and influenced new trends with his make-up laden androgynous looks and eclectic ensembles. What is name of the icon among icons who named his alter-ego Ziggy Stardust?

66.  Name the mega music star and fashion icon who collaborated with Fendi to deliver the *Fendi Prints On* capsule collection in 2019.

67.  Who is the iconic sixties model, treasured muse and collaborator of futuristic designer Rudi Gernreich, who modeled his famous topless "monokini" swimsuit in 1964?

68.  Which Canadian supermodel and muse to fame photographer Steven Meisel was voted *The Greatest Supermodel of All Time* by viewers of the *TV Show Fashion File* in 2008?

69.  The Daily Express dubbed her the *Face of '66*. Give the well-known nickname of the 1960's mod fashion model born Lesley Hornby.

70.  Which Jamaican model, actress, and singer is lauded for having one of the most iconic album covers for her 1981 album *Nightclubbing*, which featured her in her signature evocative androgynous look?

71.  She was listed amongst Forbes 2017 World's 100 Most Powerful Women. Which Indian model and actress won the *Miss World 2000* pageant?

72.  Name the Brazilian supermodel, fashion icon, and savvy business woman who published the book *Lessons: My Path to a Meaningful Life* in 2018.

౷౦౷

# 3. The Narrators: Editors, Publicists, & Writers

Level: Easy

73. Name the renowned  fashion publicist, bestselling author, and founder of the public relations firm *People's Revolution.*

74. Which beloved Vogue Italia Editor-in-Chief (1988-2016) authored the book *A Noir: The Black Book* (1998); an anthology of images celebrating the use of the color black in fashion, art, and architecture?

75. Name the famous fashion editor and design contest judge who succeeded Robbie Myers as Editor-in-Chief of Elle magazine in 2017.

76. In 2014 she was appointed as the International Vogue Editor at Condé Nast. Name the influential fashion critic who worked at The International Herald Tribune for 26 years.

77. Which former McKinsey & Co management consultant went on to create the Business of Fashion; a leading online publication featuring fashion news and analysis?

78. Name the British Vogue Editor-in-Chief who held the position of fashion director  at i-D magazine when he was only 18.

79. Name the former Editor-in-Chief of Marie Claire magazine who co-created and executive produced the reality TV show *Running in Heels (2009).*

80. Which prominent former Editor-in-Chief of French Vogue (2000-2011) became the Global Fashion Director at Harper's Bazaar in 2012?

81. Name the beloved on-air fashion design mentor who published his first style guide "A Guide to Quality, Taste, and Style" in 2007.

82. Which legendary fashion journalist was the first person-of-color to hold the position of Creative Director at Vogue (1998-2013)?

83. She is known as one of the most influential voices in fashion. Name the fashion editor who succeeded Grace Mirabella as Vogue's Editor-in-Chief in 1988.

84. Best known for her influential street-style, name the Vogue Japan editor-at-large who was appointed as the Scientific Director at the prestigious Istituto Marangoni in 2018.

~

Level: Intermediate

85. Name the Canadian model, known for her elaborate poses, who co-authored the book *Study of Pose* in 2014.

86. Which acclaimed fashion journalist with an esteemed career at The Washington Post was the first fashion writer to win a Pulitzer Prize for Criticism?

87. Name the iconic Vogue editor who succeeded the revered Diana Vreeland as Editor-in-Chief in 1971.

88. Which TV personality and mega style-influencer published her first book, *IT*, in 2013?

89. She described her editorship at Harper's Bazaar as "a long love affair". Name the legendary Harper's Bazaar editor-in-chief (1934-58) who is credited with influencing the rise to prominence of Christian Dior and Cristobal Balenciaga.

90. Which Parisian admired for her chic minimalist signature style helmed Vogue Paris from 2011 to 2021?

91. Name the Russian model who, in 2012, co-founded *The Trend Spotter*; an Australian-based online fashion and lifestyle publication.

92. The legendary Empress of Fashion; name the fashion authority who's illustrious career included; columnist & editor at Harper's Bazaar(1936-62), Editor-in-Chief at Vogue (1963-71), and curator at the Costume Institute of the Metropolitan Museum of Art(1971-85).

93. Which street-style icon, entrepreneur, and former Harper's Bazaar editor co-founded the Russian digital magazine *Buro 24/7* in 2011?

94. Only the second person to hold the tittle of Fashion Critic at the New York Times. Name the American journalist who penned the publication's unabashed fashion blog, On the Runway, until 2014.

95. Which award-winning fashion editor  lead Essence Magazine as it's Editor-in Chief from 1981 to 2000?

96. Which co-author of the well-received  book, Oliver Theyskens: She Walks in Beauty, was the first to hold the post of Fashion Editor at the Financial Times?

~

## Level: Advance

97. Name the celebrated New York fashion reporter, known for her eccentric style, who after 30 years at The Village Voice became a contributing editor at Vogue.com in 2008.

98. Which former GQ Editor-in-Chief was credited with transforming the small publication into one of the most popular men's magazines during his tenure from 1983 to 2003?

99. Who was as appointed the first British-based Editor-in-Chief of British Vogue in 1916?

100. Which revered, and to many the first fashion publicist, was appointed to the National Council on the Arts of the National Endowment for the Arts in 1965?

101. Name the beloved and highly respected fashion editor who succeeded Anna Wintour to become the British Vogue Editor-in-Chief in 1987.

102. Who founded Seventeen Magazine and served as its Editor-in-Chief from 1944-1953?

103. Known as a trailblazer in the magazine industry; name the former Essence Magazine Editor-in-Chief who became Editor-in-Chief at the American feminist publication, *Ms.* magazine, in 1992.

104. Who succeeded Michelle Lee to become the third Editor-in-Chief of Allure magazine in 2021?

105. Name the Canadian journalist who was the Editor-in-Chief at Vanity Fair from 1992-2017.

106. Who was credited with reinventing and re-energizing Cosmopolitan magazine during her astounding 32 years as its Editor-in-Chief (1965-1997)?

107. Her 17 years tenure (2000-2017) as the Editor-in-Chief of Elle (US) is one the longest in the magazine's history. Name the long-serving editor who's repertoire included working for Andy Warhol at Interview.

108. Which former Editor-in-Chief (2012-2020) of Marie Claire magazine is credited with introducing Marie Claire Power Trip, a 36-hour summit for powerful professional women?

೫೦೧೩

# 4. The Artists: Stylists, Painters, Photographers, & Illustrators

109. Name the famous surrealist artist who partnered with avant garde designer Elsa Schiaparelli to create memorable pieces such as the *Lobster Dress (1937)* and the *Tear Dress (1938)*.

110. Which former Welsh model went on to be a revered fashion stylist and creative director with a career at American Vogue which lasted over 25 years?

111. He is renowned for being a master in black and white photography and capturing the male physique. Name the photographer who captured the illusory *Madonna Mirror Kiss 1987* image.

112. Which Chicago-born stylist to the stars including Zendaya, Ariana Grande and Celine Dion, won the first CFDA Stylist of the Year Award in 2022?

113. His work includes some of the most iconic portrait and editorial photography. Name the legendary photographer who delivered mesmerizing works such as *Dovima with Elephants 1955* and *Nastassja Kinski and the Serpent 1981*.

114. Amongst her most notable editorials are a pre-famous Audrey Hepburn photographed by Richard Rutledge (1952) and Marilyn Monroe's last sitting captured by Bert Stern (1962). Name the renowned former Vogue fashion editor and stylist.

115. Which acclaimed Australian fashion illustrator drew the artwork for the best selling book, *Sex and The City,* in 2006?

116. A doyenne of fashion photography, name the revered photographer who's notable photos includes the gorgeously nude pregnant bodies of Demi Moore (1991) and Serena Williams (2017) for Vanity Fair magazine covers.

117. Name the celebrity wardrobe stylist and designer who published her second book, *Living in Style: Inspiration and Advice for Everyday Glamour* in 2014.

118. Which world-renowned fashion and portrait photographer became the first non-British royal photographer in 1989 thanks to Princess Diana's affinity for his work and personality?

119. Which former protege of Diana Vreeland styled the famous *Nastassja Kinski and the Serpent 1981* photo shoot?

120. A spearhead of the 1960s Pop Art genre, name the American artist who produced the the silkscreen painting of Marilyn Monroe known as *Marilyn Diptych 1962*.

~

## Level: Intermediate

121. She is celebrated for the unforgettable outfits from the TV series *Sex in the City*. Name the New York stylist and costume designer who won the Costume Designers Guild *Excellence in Contemporary Television* Award in 2021 and 2022 for her work on *Emily in Paris*.

122. Which Antiguan-born American stylist known for her unique designs featured in top Hip Hop videos became the Creative Director of Puma Hoops in 2020?

123. Name the celebrated Peruvian photographer who captured Vanity Fair's 1997 images of Diana, Princess of Wales.

124. Which renowned Cuban-American surrealist artist authored and illustrated *Style Dictionary* (1996)?.

125. Name the British fashion and documentary photographer who shot *The 3rd Summer of Love* editorial which was published by The Face magazine in 1990.

126. Which Hong-Kong born Canadian fashion stylist and former Elle US Creative Director starred in the fashion reality series *All On The Line* (2011-)?

127. She is a maestro in the fashion styling field with a career that has spanned over 30 years. Name the British fashion stylist who styled model Helene Fillieres for the very first cover of Self Service magazine (1995).

128. He is revered for his provocative and often nude fashion photography. Name the German-Australian photographer who published the book *Pola Woman* (1992); a book filled with Polaroids, his preferred medium.

129. She has made the Hollywood Reporter 25 Most Powerful Stylist list numerous times. Name the American Stylist who served as a panelist at the 2016 E! Style Collective event and won a Marie Claire Image Maker Award in 2017.

130. Which admired fashion and nature photographer was credited with discovering the supermodel Iman in her native country of Kenya in 1975?

131. Acclaimed for his evocative images for Vogue and Vogue Italia; name the American photographer who shot the cover photo as well as other images in Madonna's New York Times bestselling book, *Sex* (1992).

132. He has collaborated with industry greats such as Rimmel London, Kylie Cosmetics, and Missguided. Name the self-taught British fashion illustrator who designed the 2018 Collector line of Bratz dolls.

~

133. Dubbed the "Father of photography", name the pioneering Luxembourgish America photographer who served as the chief photographer for  Conde Nast (Vogue, Vanity Fair) from 1923-1938.

134. Which former German model turned photographer shot the album covers of Janet Jackson's *The Velvet Rope* (1997), Dido's *Life for Rent* (2003), and Britney Spears' *Blackout* (2007)?

135. Her list of clientele includes Time Magazine,  Apple, and Marie Claire. Name the British artist who illustrated *The Little Book of Feminist Saints* (2018).

136. One of America's greatest photographers renowned for his breathtaking fashion photography, portraitures, and printmaking. Name the photographer who's striking black and white image titled *Harlequin Dress* (1979) sold for $355,600 at an April 2023 auction.

137. Which sought-after British fashion photographer shot the album cover of Madonna's *American Life* (2003) and co-directed Rihanna's *Kiss it Better* music video (2016)?

138. You may recognize his signature art deco style on the covers of vintage copies of Vogue and Vanity Fair. Name the French artist who's illustrated the iconic book, *Les Choses de Paul Poiret* (1911).

139. Which German photographer and photojournalist known for her glamorous and elegant aesthetics, created the ethereal *Butterfly Series Blue 1974* photo; a double exposed color photo with blue butterfly wings softly encircling the model's face?

140. His work was provocative and innovative. Name the surrealistic French photographer behind the legs-only 1979 photo advertising campaign for Charles Jourdan shoe company.

141. Which Korean-Australian illustrator, known for his enchanting watercolors and *Susu Girls*, collaborated with Lancôme for the beauty brand's Spring/Summer 2017 Paris inspired campaign?

142. Name the renowned British fashion photographer who directed Lady Gaga's visually stunning music video for *Born This Way* (2011).

143. He is known for his elegant portraits of high society, including the British Royal Family. Name the British photographer who won the Academy Award for Best Costume Design (1964) for the splendid ensembles worn in *My Fair Lady*.

144. He is celebrated for his contributions to the creation of Essence magazine and serving as its first editorial director from 1970-1973. Name the photographer who was the first African American to shoot for Vogue and Life magazine.

₧₧

# 5. The Lingo: Words, Terms, & Idioms

Level: Easy

145. Traditionally made of wood and used as protective footwear, what type of ancient slip-on, backless shoes made a modern resurgence as Crocs?

146. The Gucci *Diana*, Hermès *Birkin*, and Louis Vuitton *Neverfull* are all examples of what type of bag?

147. A short-lived fashion trend is known as a?

148. Similar to the trumpet which has a flare starting at the hip, this type of wedding gown features a flare that starts at the knee.

149. Anna Wintour's signature bob is an example of which hairstyle worn by young men in medieval times?

150. This French phrase literally translate to "in the current fashion".

151. Fishtail, cornrow, and flat twist are all achieved using which hairstyling technique?

152. A line of stitches used to secure two pieces of fabric is known as a?

153. The scents that make up a fragrance olfactory pyramid such as vanilla and musk are called the?

154. What is the English term used to describe clothing that the French refer to as pret-a-porter?

155. The runway used by models to display clothes at fashion shows is known as a?

156. Poor boy, dolman, and raglan are all types of?

157. This extra-large pocket is named after an Australian marsupial and is placed on center-front of a garment such as a sweatshirt.

158. The rope-soled shoe with a canvas upper that originated in Spain is known as an?

~

Level: Intermediate

159. Dating back to Ancient China, which type of ornamental fastener uses braid or cording to create a knot-button and loop closure?

160. The type of fibre derived from the Angora goat's coat is called?

161. The portion of a hat that covers the top of the head is called the ?

162. Designer Christian Lacroix made which puffed-up and crumpled skirt popular in the 80's?

163. The second line of a high-end fashion brand such as Versace's Versus is known as a ?

164. Inspired by Venetian masks, Altina Schinasi designed which shape of women eyewear which was popular in the 1930s?

165. Sometimes used to identify a type of women's riding coat, what is the French word for skirt?

166. In 1962, Sonia Rykiel, the *Queen of Knit*, introduced which fitted, rib-knit, striped sweater?

167. What term is used to describe a garment with an informal balance wherein one side of the garment is not the same as the other such as a slanted hemline or a one-shoulder bodice?

168. What unit of mass is used to measure the weight of precious stones?

169. A fiber that is not derived from a natural materials and is man-made/artificially created is known as a?

170. How do you call someone who makes or deals specifically with the trade of women hats?

171. A ring set with a single stone such as a diamond or a sapphire gemstone is known as a?

172. Unlike the umbrella which is meant to protect the user from precipitation, which folding convex canopy accessory is used as a protection from the sun?

~

Level: Advance

173. The study of footwear in areas such as archeology and fashion history is known as?

174. Which traditional dress worn by the women of Hawaii was introduced to their culture by missionaries who wore similar styles from the Empire period?

175. Cashmere produced from the hair of the Kashmir goat in the Kashmir region is known as?

176. What word, derived from Italian pasta, was used in Britain to describe the ostentatious French and Italian influenced fashion of aristocratic young men in the 1760's-1770's?

177. What is the last stage of the fashion cycle when customer interest has waned and the product is considered outdated?

178. Unlike vintage which refers to original clothing articles from the past, what term is used to describe current, updated versions of past styles?

179. Popular in the 50's and 60's, a small tuft of facial hair worn by men just below their lower lip is call a?

180. Fashioned from the pants worn by Spanish bullfighters, which women below-the-knee, tight-fitting pants were popular in the 60's?

181. Similar to couture, what term is used in menswear to describe a suit which has been custom-made (as opposed to off-the-rack) to the specification of the client's measurements and preferences?

182. Which textile is produced using a knotting technique that dates back to ancient times?

183. In menswear, the difference between the waist and chest measurements of a jacket is known as?

184. Similar to gold-plating, which jewelry gilding technique covers sterling or pure silver with a thick layer of gold?

185. Originating from seamen's need for clothing to wear on land, which 16th-19th century version of today's ready-to-wear stores sold cheap, poor fitting garments?

186. A tradition Japanese straw-soled thong sandals akin to the flip-flop is known as a?

ॐ

# 6. The Institutions: Events, Museums, & Organizations

Level: Easy

187. Which magazine began selecting and announcing the recipient of the *Sexiest Man Alive* title since 1985?

188. Name the famous shoe museum located in Toronto, Canada which is located in a unique building designed by Moriyama & Teshima Architects.

189. Name the London-based public art and design university which boasts these notable alumni, Sade Adu, Alexander McQueen, John Galliano, and Stella McCartney.

190. Known for it's Brown Bags and spectacular window displays, name the luxury department store founded in New York 1861 by a father and son duo.

191. Which popular men's magazine was formerly named Apparel Art (1931-57)?

192. A protected heritage building, name the upscale Oxford Street department store that served as a bomb shelter and bunker for a secret scrambling machine during World War II.

193. Name the leading fashion magazine which was first published in New York in 1867. It's debut issue featured illustrations of *Fall Bonnets* and *Bridal Toilets*.

194. Which mega shopping mall, with over 1200 stores, is located adjacent to the megastructure which claimed the world record for tallest building in 2009?

195. It started as a fundraising event for the museum in 1948, but has evolved into a celebrity fashion extravaganza. Name the event which theme was *Karl Lagerfeld: A Line of Beauty* in 2023.

196. Located in Knightsbridge, name the London luxury emporium and iconic landmark which introduced the city's first moving staircase (escalator) in 1898.

~

## Level: Intermediate

197. Which non-profit American fashion trade association was founded by Eleanor Lambert in 1962?

198. When this men's fashion magazine was purchased by Condé Montrose Nast in 1912 it was named *Simply Dress*. What is it called today?

199. Thanks to the sponsorship of CHANEL, which renowned City of Paris fashion museum converted it cellars to create the Gabrielle Chanel Galleries (opened in 2020)?

200. Which museum has organized the annual *Dress of the Year* award since 1963?

201. Name the leading Australian luxury department store, known for its houndstooth branding, which was founded by a Welsh business man in Sidney, Australia in 1838.

202. Name the fashion organization that has honored top icons and creatives in fashion at their annual *Night of Stars* gala  since 1983.

203. Sometimes referred to as the *Bible of Fashion*, name the fashion trade journal created by John Fairchild that has been in operation for over a century.

204. Housed in a building shaped like a bag, which handbag museum located in Seoul, Korea opened  its doors to the public in July, 2012?

205. In 1940 Eleanor Lambert started the International Best Dressed List. As of 2002 which American magazine was charged with curating this list?

206. Still referred to by many as *Fashion's Oscars*, name the American fashion award that handed out *Winnies* to top American designers from 1942-1984.

~

Level: Advance

207. It is dedicated to collecting, conserving, and researching Western fashion; name the fashion institute founded in Japan in 1978.

208. Which iconic shopping gallery and architectural marvel located in Milan, was constructed between 1865 and 1867, and is named after the first king of Italy?

209. Which London-based museum acquired 300 early punk and New Romantic pieces from the private collection of fashion impresarios Michael and Gerlinde Costiff in 2002?

210. A mainstay in men's fashion, which menswear fashion trade fair, held bi-annually in Florence, was established in 1972?

211. Which fashion institution organizes The Fashion Awards, an annual ceremony held in the United Kingdom since 1989?

212. In 1893 Theophile Bader and Alphonso Kahn opened a 750 square feet store in Paris. Name the French *"luxury bazaar"* which grew to over 700,000 square feet and operates its flagship on the famous Boulevard Haussmann.

213. Which company, appreciated in the design world for its color matching system, has been announcing the *Color of The Year* since 1999?

214. This company has grown into one of the most well-known sewing machine brands. Name the sewing machine manufacturer that was founded in New York in 1851.

215. It began as a small tailor's shop acquired by Ramón Areces Rodríguez in    Madrid in 1935. Name Spain's leading department store chain which is easily recognized by its green and white logo.

216. A favorite among fashion designers and manufacturers, name the zipper company which originated in Japan as San-es Shokai in 1934.

∞⌘∞

# 7. The Moments: Influential, Memorable, & Momentous

*This chapter is arranged in chronological order.*

217. *1783.* In the Elisabeth Vigee-Lebrun painting Marie Antonétte is wearing a *Robe de Gaulle* made out of which fabric that sparked a controversy at the time?

218. *1926.* Coco Chanel introduces what fashion item to the world in Vogue's October issue?

219. *1954.* Karl Lagerfeld began his apprenticeship as which designer's assistant?

220. *1955.* Which Marilyn Monroe film features the famous movie still of her in a white dress over a subway grate?

221. *1956.* Which iconic handbag, initially called *Sac à Dépêches,* was renamed after the Princess of Monaco?

222. *1961.* In the opening scene of the iconic film *Breakfast at Tiffany's* Audrey Hepburn wore which accessory designed by Oliver Goldsmith?

223. *1961.* Jackie Kennedy wore 3 striking accessories to her husband's inauguration; elbow gloves, a fur hand muff, and a *what* designed by Roy Halston Frowick?

224. *1964.* Carroll Baker wore a transparent "nude"dress made by which luxury brand to the premiere of *The Carpetbaggers*?

225. *1966.* Which designer presented the *Le Smoking* tuxedo suit for women?

226. *1970*. Bob Mackie designed a crystal bodysuit worn on the cover of which music icon's *Everything is Everything* album.

227. *1974*. Beverly Johnson was the first black cover star of which magazine?

228. *1975*. Which singer wore a sequin LA Dodgers baseball unitard to perform at his Dodgers stadium concert?

229. *1976*. Calvin Klein was the first designer to show *what* on the runway?

230. *1977*. John Travolta wore a white three piece suit featuring what type of popular 70's pants in the movie *Saturday Night Fever*?

231. *1984*. Nike debuted  which basketball star's signature sneaker line?

232. *1985*. Which hairstyle did Grace Jone wear in the classic James Bond film *A View to Kill*?

233. *1990*. In Episode 2 of Season 1 of *The Fresh Prince of Bel Air*, Will Smith wore a pair of Zebra striped pants from which brand?

234. *1990*. The Face June issue featured photographs of Kate Moss wearing the Palermo and Rio styles of which brand of sandals?

235. *1995*. In the film *Clueless* the lead character, Cher Horowitz, wore a yellow suit featuring which pattern?

236. *1998.* Alexander McQueen used robotic arms at his fashion show to spray paint a white dress on which model?

237. *2001.* Bjork wore a dress to the 73rd Academy Awards that was in the likeness of which feathered friend?

238. *2002.* Halle Berry won an Oscar wearing a gown with a sheer embroidered top and deep red taffeta skirt designed by which designer?

239. *2002.* Lindsay Lohan wore flip-flops paired with a green velour tracksuit by which brand to the Children's Choice Awards?

240. *2003.* Which brand of sheepskin boots made the *Oprah's Favorite Things* list?

241. *2009.* Actress Kristen Stewart paired her red Yigal Azrouel taffeta dress with which brand of sneakers at the MTV Movie Awards?

242. *2010.* Who designed Lady Gaga's meat suit for the MTV Video Music Awards?

243. *2011.* At the Venice Film Festival Kate Winslet wore a white and black, figure-flattering body-con dress by which designer?

244. *2015.* To attend the Grammy Awards Taylor Swift paired her ombre teal-blue Elie Saab gown with which designer bright pink platform wedge sandals?

245. *2015.* Which hairstyle did Zendaya wear to the 87<sup>th</sup> Academy Awards?

246. *2017.* Jacquemus debuted which line of micro handbags?

247. *2020.* Then democratic vice-president candidate, Kamala Harris, wore which brand of boots to visit the aftermath of a California wildfire?

248. *2021.* Beyonce posted photos on her instagram wearing a white, mid-size, vegan leather, "always sold-out" shopper from which brand?

249. *2021.* Which National Youth Poet Laureate wore a kente cloth gown on the cover of Vogue?

250. *2023.* To perform at the Super Bowl half-time show Rihanna wore a custom-made red flight suit and leather corset made by which brand?

୫୬

## The Answers

**1. The Creators: Designers, Couturiers, & Legends**

1.   Christian Dior
2.   Olivier Rousteing
3.   Donatella Versace
4.   Valentino Garavani
5.   Gabrielle (Coco) Chanel
6.   Jason Wu
7.   Diane von Furstenburg
8.   Azzedine Alaia
9.   Alexander McQueen
10.   Karl Lagerfeld
11.   Jean Paul Gaultier
12.   Betsey Johnson
13.   Hubert de Givenchy
14.   Daniel "Dapper Dan" Day
15.   Ralph Lauren
16.   Donna Karan
17.   Stella Jean
18.   Main Rousseau Bocher (Mainbocher)
19.   Tom Ford
20.   Ann Lowe
21.   Stella McCartney
22.   Yohji Yamamoto

23. Elsa Schiaparelli

24. Virgil Abloh

25. Martin Margiela

26. Jeanne Lanvin

27. Charles Frederick Worth

28. Rudolf Rudi Gernreich

29. Iris van Herpen

30. Paul Poiret

31. Callot Soeurs (Callot Sisters)

32. Gabrielle "Gaby" Aghion

33. Yves Saint Laurent

34. Miuccia Prada

35. Pierre Cardin

36. Dorothea Noelle Naomi "Thea" Porter

## 2.The Influencers: Icons, Models, & Muses

37. Halima Aden

38. Cara Delevingne

39. Gigi Hadid

40. Michelle Obama

41. Princess Diana

42. Michael Jackson

43. Jackie Kennedy Onassis

44. Rihanna
45. Grace Kelly
46. Audrey Hepburn
47. Kimora Lee Leissner (prev. Simons nee Perkins)
48. Kendell Jenner
49. Isabella Blow
50. James Dean
51. Lady Gaga
52. Lucy Douglas "C.Z." Guest
53. Naomi Campbell
54. Jane Birkin
55. Tyra Banks
56. Marilyn Monroe
57. Kate Moss
58. Iman
59. Harry Styles
60. Ashley Graham
61. Bettina Graziani
62. Zendaya
63. Aimee Mullins
64. Heidi Klum
65. David Bowie
66. Nicki Minaj

67. Peggy Monffitt

68. Linda Evangelista

69. Twiggy

70. Grace Jones

71. Priyanka Chopra

72. Gisele Bündchen

## 3.The Narrators: Editors, Publicists, & Writers

73. Kelly Cutrone

74. Franca Sozzani

75. Nina Garcia

76. Suzy Menkes

77. Imran Ahmed

78. Edward Enninful

79. Joanna Coles

80. Carine Roitfeld

81. Tim Gunn

82. Andre Leon Talley

83. Anna Wintour

84. Anna della Russo

85. Coco Rocha

86. Robin Givhan

87. Grace Mirabella

88. Alexa Chung
89. Carmel Snow
90. Emmanuelle Alt
91. Dasha Gold
92. Diana Vreeland
93. Miroslava Duma
94. Cathy Horyn
95. Susan L. Taylor
96. Vanessa Friedman
97. Lynn Yaeger
98. Art Cooper
99. Elspeth Champcommunal
100. Eleanor Lambert
101. Elizabeth 'Liz' Tilberis
102. Helen Valentine
103. Marcia Ann Gillespie
104. Jessica Cruel
105. Graydon Carter
106. Helen Gurley Brown
107. Roberta "Robbie" Myers
108. Anne Fulenwider

## 4. The Artists: Stylists, Painters, Photographers, & Illustrators

109.  Salvadore Dali

110. Grace Coddington

111. Bruce Weber

112. Law Roach

113. Richard Avedon

114. Baps Simpson

115. Megan Hess

116. Annie Leibovitz

117. Rachel Zoe

118. Patrick Dermachelier

119. Polly Allen Mellen

120. Andy Warhol

121. Patricia Field

122. June Ambrose

123. Mario Testino

124. Ruben Toledo

125. Corinne Day

126. Joe Zee

127. Jane How

128. Helmut Newton

129. Cristina Ehrlich

130. Peter Beard

131. Steven Meisel

132. Hayden Williams

133. Edward Steichen

134. Ellen von Unweath

135. Manjit Thapp

136. Irving Penn

137. Craig McDean

138. Georges Lapape

139. Regina Relang

140. Guy Bourdin

141. JaeSuk Kim

142. Nick Knight

143. Cecil Beaton

144. Gordon Parks

## 5. The Lingo: Words, Terms, & Idioms

145. Clogs

146. Tote

147. Fad

148. Mermaid

149. Pageboy

150. A la mode

151. Braiding/Plaiting

152. Seam

153. Notes

154. Ready-to-wear

155. Catwalk

156. Sleeves

157. Kangaroo

158. Espadrille

159. Frog/Olivette

160. Mohair

161. Crown

162. Le Pouf/Pouf Skirt

163. Diffusion line/ Bridge Line

164. Harlequin Frame/Harlequin Glasses

165. Jupe

166. Poorboy Sweater

167. Asymmetric

168. Carat

169. Synthetic Fiber

170. Milliner

171. Solitaire

172. Parasol

173. Calceology

174. Holoku

175. Pashmina

176. Macaroni

177. Obsolescence

178. Retro

179. Soul Patch

180. Toreador

181. Bespoke

182. Macrame

183. Drop

184. Gold Vermeil

185. Slop Shop

186. Zori

## 6. The Institutions: Events, Museums, & Organizations

187. People Magazine

188. Bata Shoe Museum

189. Central Saint Martins College of Art and Design

190. Bloomingdales

191. GQ

192. Selfridges

193. Harper's Bazaar

194. Dubai Mall

195. Met Gala/ Met Ball

196. Harrods

197. Council of Fashion Designers of America (CFDA)

198. Vanity Fair

199. Palais Galliera

200. Fashion Museum, Bath

201. David Jones

202. Fashion Group International (FGI)

203. Women's Wear Daily (WWD)

204. Simone Handbag Museum

205. Vanity Fair

206. Coty Fashion Awards

207. Kyoto Costume Institute

208. Galleria Vittorio Emanuele II

209. Victoria and Albert Museum (V&A)

210. Peitti Immagine Uomo

211. British Fashion Council

212. Galeries Lafayette

213. Pantone LLC

214. Singer

215. El Corte Inglés

216. YKK

## 7. The Moments: Influential, Memorable, & Momentous

217. Cotton Muslin

218. Little Black Dress (LBD)

219. Pierre Balmain

220. The Seven Year Itch

221. Hermes Kelly

222. Sunglasses

223. Pillbox Hat

224. Balmain

225. Yves Saint Laurent

226. Diana Ross

227. American Vogue

228. Elton John

229. Jeans

230. Bell-bottom/Flared

231. Michael Jordan

232. Flattop

233. Zubaz

234. Birkenstock

235. Plaid

236. Shalom Harlow

237. Swan

238. Elie Saab

239. Juicy Couture

240. UGG

241. Converse Chuck Taylor

242. Franc Fernandez

243. Stella McCartney

244. Giuseppe Zanotti

245. Dreadlocks

246. Le Chiquito

247. Timberlands

248. Telfar

249. Amanda Gorman

250. Loewe

෴

# *About the Author*

Ree van Dijk is a fashion consultant and writer who is committed to enhancing lives through the transformative power of style. Armed with an in-depth knowledge of fashion and notable experience in image consulting, Ree has developed image management solutions that inspire a culture of style, substance, and success. She is a steadfast believer that functional elegance is the key to mastering life and its many intricacies.

Ree has a Master of Fine Arts in Fashion Merchandising and Management from the acclaimed Academy of Art University of San Francisco. She also obtained her certification in Image Consulting at the prestigious Fashion Institute of Technology of New York.

Ree wrote Fun Fashion Trivia for all who desire an engaging way in which to challenge their knowledge on the delightful world of fashion.

For more fun fashion trivia questions visit **reevandijk.com**

# From the Author

*Dear Reader,*

*Thank you so much for purchasing Fun Fashion Trivia!*

*I hope you enjoy testing your knowledge on all things fashion. If you have a spare moment, I would greatly appreciate it if you could leave a review on the platform where you purchased this book. Your feedback is incredibly valuable to me and helps other fashion and trivia aficionados discover my work.*

*Thank you again for your support!*

*Ree van Dijk*

*Contact:*
*Website: reevandik.com*
*Email: info@reevandijk.com*